Also by Nicholas A. Price

Poetry Books

AN ELEPHANT IN MY FRONT YARD: *AND OTHER OBSERVATIONS*

THOUGHTS OF YOU: *AND OTHER LOVE POEMS*

BRIDGES TO MANHATTAN: *AND OTHER POETIC JOURNEYS*

Fine Art Photography Books

CLEARED HOT!

PLAYGROUND OF THE GODS

HISTORIC ICONS

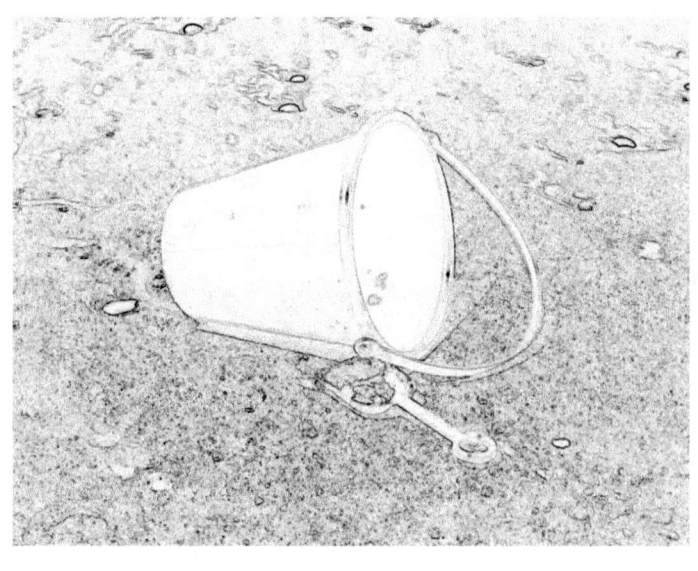

FORGOTTEN HOLIDAY
and other poems

by

Nicholas A. Price

A Tough Tribe Book

FORGOTTEN HOLIDAY: *AND OTHER POEMS*
A Tough Tribe Book
Copyright © 2011 Nicholas A. Price

Cover design by S. J. Harris

Cover images and internal illustrations courtesy of Nicholas A. Price ©
2005-2010. All rights reserved

Library of Congress Catalogue in Publication Data on file with the
publisher

If you purchased this book without a cover, you should be aware that
this book is stolen property. It was reported as "unsold and
destroyed" to the publisher and neither the author nor the publisher
has received any payment for this "stripped book".

All Rights Reserved. Reproduction in part or whole is strictly prohibited
No part of this publication may be reproduced, stored in a retrieval
system, or transmitted in any form or by any means, electronic,
mechanical, photo-copying, recording or otherwise, without the prior
consent of the publisher and the author.

First Edition
ISBN 978-0-9798390-5-4
Produced in NEW YORK
Printed and published in the USA
www.ToughTribe.com

OPM 10 9 8 7 6 5 4 3 2 1

TITLE	PAGE
Forgotten Holiday	*13*
Dream Coast	*15*
Aching Legs	*17*
Off the Mains	*18-19*
Away from the Valley of Darkness	*21*
Empty Sunday	*23*
Island Mother	*25*
The Promise of Aldenham	*27*
Bridges of Iron	*29*
Kings to Berwick	*31*
Ancient Proximity	*33*
No Fixed Abode	*35*
Freedom	*37*
High Street Hopes	*39*
Little Sea and Last Ditches	*41*
No Coals	*43*

Another Yawning Morning	*45*
The Winding Frome	*47*
Horace and the Lifting Bridge	*49*
Mythical Titans	*51*
Sahra to Sahel	*53*
Scrumping	*55*
Loch Life	*57*
Mud and Shale	*59*
Semi-detached	*61*
Rhondda	*63*
The Auction	*65*
Mountain View	*67*
Troubled Father	*69*
Ivorian Hope	*71*
The King's Daughter	*73*
The Smoke	*75*

Ship Canals and Red Bricks	*77*
Three Hundred and Ninety Nine	*78-79*
The Guardian	*81*
Tar and Tie	*83*
The Sitting Room	*85*
The Unyielding Zebra	*87*
The Harbor	*89*
Relegated to the Guards Van	*91*

ABOUT THE AUTHOR

Forgotten Holiday

She rested empty by the sea,
A lofty white monstrosity,
Yellowing stains of a bygone age,
Barred doors to drinking bars,
Running dry every Sunday,
A weeded reception,
A cigarette paper past,
Headlines under foot,
Barracked bodies waiting,
Ready rubbed, tinned tobacco,
Dog ends and hair cream trails,
Rotten plans and rusted safes,
Persistent nineteen thirties green,
Structured rust, mottled walls,
Fading curtains and ebbing carpets,
A constant gale force volley,
Throwing the shore grit airborne,
Sandy heaps climbing daily,
A monumental growth spree disguised,
Beneath the reaching, wiry jade whispers,
A tripping Morris, wood and moss,
A stalled Austin, forgotten Rover,
A Ford or two, parked on the slant,
Enjoying a corrosive breeze,
The tide washing far off beaches,
Touching a distant brushed edge,
Now the waves had deserted her too.

Dream Coast

Leaving the rattling chains, broken haven roads,
Troubling the training bank, tarnishing beacons,
Racing with shoals at the feet of Old Harry,
His belated wife below,
Chancing a trip through Durdle Door,
On an unruffled day,
Making parallel progress,
Channel lapped concordant rock,
Chewed by waved water, infinite sea banter,
Sculpting coves and flaring ingresses, a dream coast,
Crumpling stairs to a thrashing watery path,
Earthly black holes and chewed chalky drops,
Sandwich strata backdrops, the past laid down,
Greensand and Portland, wrestling a spring surge,
Opposing gulls and a badly battered catch,
The followers glance nervously,
Edging Scratchy's Bottom, plunging effortlessly,
Landed gentry to unlocked water,
Past escapades concealed, Man O war bay,
Broken vestiges scattered, upon spiny limestone backs,
The cutting deep crumbling high white rises,
Jurassic nesting cliffs, slipping into Lyme bay,
Carted away, to some long shore beach,
Quickly restored to castles, on a balmy summer day.

Aching Legs

Reverberation rolled over,
Those impossible bricked arches,
Curling into the air, compacted mortar and moss glue,
Austere pillboxes standing,
Stranded in the berry thorn garden,
Never reaching, the grounding daggers hanging,
Foot long nails gripping soot black sky,
An abbreviated existence, as tall transport slips by,
No reciprocation beneath,
Lumbering boot black rubber feet,
Sidings in space, transmitting loaded directions,
Blank buffet cars, fuming city passengers,
Eating the scenery towards the unkempt meadows,
Lost to brackish water and retired boating planks,
Craving respite in streaming wheeled boxes,
Lifting the weight from reluctant leaden feet,
Counting the endless linden line,
Dapper trimmed to perfection,
Drawn by the familiar hum of
meandering travel machines,
Red bell pushes, the jangle of bagged cash,
Hand wound tickets, pennies for a ride,
Passing requested stops, misplaced in between,
Heading to the hazy distant horizon with aching legs,
The promise of a smooth journey home.

Off the Mains

The thirty-three hurled sulfur into the upper air,
Leaving the smoke and mains behind her,
Breathing in liberated space,
Snorting with freedoms chortle,
Prepared for a hearty slog to the seashore,
Dreaming of steering independence,
Rusting, risky shell collecting adventures,
Frequent leisurely afternoons,
Drawing patterns in the sand with iron feet,
Winding through history and holiday hopes,
Those miniature towns, where people lived, little else,
Over the strips of skeletal territory,
Fording brackish backwaters and stranded fish,
Sleeping vessels resting at forty-five,
Waiting for change,
Drifting past destruction, cut by the doctors axe,
Glancing underground, overgrown closures,
Thorny sidings, not stopping,
Tree ghosts standing, platform waiting,

Onward to Roman promise and a colorful dreamscape,
Surging emerald rolls and lambs for slaughter,
Barreling the chalky rise,
Etchings of a contemporary giant,
Skirting around the hillside and pagan monsters,
Swiftly drifting upon the downgrade,
Sighted promises of washed beaches,
Abundant lovers, with ample time,
Enveloped chips, strewn chairs and famished gulls,
Those iconic knot headed trippers, sunning for a week,
Tightly stacked in guesthouse hideaways,
Bed, breakfast, color television and a sea view,
Obediently waiting for a jaunt with the bored donkeys.

Away from the Valleys of Darkness

Rolling greens rumbled towards the sea,
Cleansing waves folding,
The perpendicular face of mother,
Angled strata shelves, emerging from the sands,
The craggy hideaways of daughters,
The clinging roots of father,
Plated crumpled hollows,
Long lost brothers slowly devoured,
Grandfather defeated, ashen stick eroded,
Falling to a sudden death, storm felled rock,
Crushed by gravity, a slaughtered generation,
Evading supervision and squandering offspring,
Cloaked by gorse air perfume, far off lavender,
Lives lacking intrusion,
Warring for a once grateful nation,
Returning forgotten, to some pastoral outpost,
A threadbare band, stamped metal,
Valleys of darkness, the only thanks.

Empty Sunday

Another drained Sunday left me cold,
Lamenting your warm clogged vessels,
The whine of work forsaken,
Sailing weekends, wadding white islands,
Parting timed vaults, access denied,
Not a penny piece, in a cobbled crack or closer,
Dropping percentages, sapped each day,
For umbrella pinstripes and walking cases,
Stock and share banter, pink paper,
Flat lining graphs, awaiting returning patients,
Kindred kitchens and blind post boxes,
Letters only halfway,
Resting dust cylinders, no announcements,
Newspapers stringed, knifed at dawn,
The Guardian and Gay Times with cornered coffee,
Butchering barbers and a city cut,
Top shelf girls, something for the weekend,
Executive contours and neat at the sides,
Royal exchanges with threaded needles,
Bursting bullion and swarming stairs,
Ant tracks and a square mile echoes.

Island Mother

Stalled windmills scattered the land,
Undulating boards of broken game pieces,
Wings sliding over desolate outcrops,
Rolling with impeded seas, thrown back to the straits,
Daydreaming of Scottish shores,
Secreted submarines, rivaling ravenous nets,
Snagging scowling trawlers,
Tree-bending air unremitting,
Twisting eternity out of shape,
In the chosen prevailing direction,
Grassy hill builders and stone stackers,
Governing the humble, enfolded sheep,
Outnumbering all and defenseless,
Evading summer flies, rusted woolen clippers,
Carted and boxed for a spring day out,
Across the gaunt bridge,
Passed by the jovial Irish, galloping home,
Holyhead and onward to emerald anticipation,
Slipping past the distressed dunes,
Boxes of misplaced dreams,
City dodging affluent hideaways,
Weeping of losses in sausage castles,
Distant tides shifting the shore, further each day,
Time carefully washing the restful beach.

The promise of Aldenham

Running red boxes rolled with exhausted clatter,
Years in a row stop and start,
Plying the hardened black tar,
Cheerful prizes in a dull world,
Swept up old reels and trapped tickets,
Fine gray ash dropped from above,
Miniature love notes scribbled,
On the way home from school,
Adolescent love seated, larger than life in the mirror,
Upstairs of course, fighting the smoke,
Grown up and away from staring eyes,
Grannies and too many bags,
Seething throngs of restless children,
Weary mothers with empty purses,
Jaundiced ceilings, white downstairs,
Amusement until the conductor coughed,
Winding his silver machine,
Rattling the leather satchel, spilling sullied coins,
Routed a thousand times and several lavatory doors,
Never stopping for rinsing refurbishment,
Switched and substituted with new swatches and tires,
Sent satisfaction and splendid hope,
One hundred and fifty thousand miles,
Forty a week, one every hour,
Conveying souls and buses,
Slatted wood clogged, pavement dirt and downpour,
Space for awkward prams and sodden umbrellas,
Bell pushes and restricted drivers.

Bridges of Iron

Striding bold ellipses crossed
the causeway of watery weeds,
Mirrored past glories, puzzled pot poachers,
Feuding charcoal fusers, cleaving departed forests,
Black fossils spooned from the caked surface,
Effortless alchemy, pigs in a row,
Leaving bricked up bones, corroded crucibles,
Filling a molten space, jam-packed,
Blackberry thorns, nitrogenous nettles,
Chopping mowers and aimless welted pickers,
Weeping ancestors reminisce, wrought wheels rolling,
Sweltering plates, the hiss of broken men,
Industrial revolutionaries,
Sunless sheds and satanic heat,
Carting riches from oaken promise,
Parting with a pocked façade of alien pines,
Neatly ornate structures, time standing witnesses,
Fragrant flaming ore, graceless in space,
Contented consumers, substituted metal,
Incessant ringing, sentry-banked phones,
The scripted sounds of an overplayed yarn,
Faded splendor and dismantled iron.

Kings to Berwick

Deserting the humpbacked sheds,
Heading out on a plate of iron spaghetti,
Spread towards the confusing north,
Past the triple gas jar silhouettes,
Glancing at the locks of a watery past,
Catching fleeting color glimpses,
Streetwalkers on a lattice link,
Forgetting the tight knit weave of city life,
Taking the fastest way out,
Hopping over river and canal,
Drilling through those obstinate hills,
Coursing for the dropping coast,
Tasting a cold easterly breeze,
Yearning for the straddling border bridge,
Berwick beckons, twisting along the precipice,
Steep cliffs leaving you green,
No need to join the undulating sea,
Embracing the coast of waterlogged voyages,
Departed kings and Nordic shores,
Crossing the ramparts with anticipation,
The final sliver, primeval promises of Waverley,
Volcanic black fortresses, upland resources,
A hunger for more, the sorrel calling,
Pledging reassurance, clattering across the forth,
Navigating the ancient backbone,
Uniting with the strength of the clans.

Ancient Proximity

Forgotten barefoot children, battle barbwire weeds,
Parents float on another psychedelic trip, over the sun,
Wading through the lake of trance, absent senses,
Hard driven vans transformed,
Unforgiving second homes,
Redundant color patches, off the dusty bargain shelf,
Covering commercial scrawl,
Enticing a passing public,
Roofed condensation, a rousing sunrise shower,
Clammy coach conversions, religious intentions,
Proud displays, bizarre listings,
The amateur chemist collection,
Faithful sheets, borrowed from another time,
Suffocating soft summer meadows,
Synthetic cloaks of death,
Naked day-trippers open, in the path of two-stroke air,
The mysterious stones
forever rising from verdant ground,
Primeval permanence, uniformly fenced,
Battling besieged earth and scattered society,
Fleeting occupation, in ancient proximity.

No Fixed Abode

Bark born circles bear down on mossy earth,
Suffocating needle carpets, soften the approach,
Parting a course through budding broom,
Breaching the primordial bracken,
Toppling workers heaps, stimulating sentinels,
Subtracting Adders, engaging stags in fighting folly,
Misjudged under running feet, dealt a hefty blow,
Barrage barbs scratching every passer,
Cones carry on searching, for a basic resting place,
Despising those ranks of organized chaos,
Two up and two down,
Making room for gleaming silver white,
Clinging to a temporary space,
Standing still, moving at a moment's notice,
For wind brushed inferno or applied writ,
Soon finding one more embryonic place,
No fixed abode, upon this owned earth.

Freedom

Fresh dew cooled our morning soft feet,
Scampering over a spongy lime lawn,
Let loose, the world was ours,
Summoning soft invading sand,
Breaching the bubbling sea,
Spiraling silken surf,
Catching the iridescent water,
Preparing for a distant future,
Salt wind tussling our hair,
Whimsical gulls fooling,
Tumbling and gliding,
Long afternoons and backwater,
Muddy time memories marked,
Our fleeting washed footprints,
Fearless miniature ships, into the deep,
Life percolated past unnoticed,
A small stream flowing,
Through an hourglass of existence,
Narrow and focused, one grain at a time,
Any doubt, posted with the past,
Moments never counted,
Freedom, I remember it well.

High Street Hopes

My memories are alive,
Walking along the simple High Street, tall curbs,
Narrow pavements, sluggish buses each way,
Almost scraping,
Fishy windows and sawdust butchers, escaping,
Sugar bread and cobblers leather, cakes piled high,
Stinking department stores, flying bagged cash,
Long hardware waits, buckled wooden floors,
Old pennies,
Noisy hinges and roll up smoke, snuffed
without a care, rarely looking up at the stripped sky,
Suicide windows and collapsing oyster banks,
Post office pensions, over licked stamps, Thursdays,
With fresh milled air and childish puppets tapping,
Barbershop balm, spinning signs,
A short back and sides,
Turning to the quayside of vigilant rye pigeons,
Pecking,
Ample fish and tobacco windows, news on the wind,
Fat cats slipping through impossible gaps,
Running rodents,
Rows of banned buildings,
Tracking cranes and laden coasters,
Lofty gulls and ragged worms, neatly sliced,
Broken pottery and stranded hulls,
Awaiting seasonal paint,
It seems so painless to overlook today.

Little Sea and Last Ditches

Corrugated cafes and slatted sides,
The length of the little sea reaches,
Nudists and last French ditches,
Ridge walkers, plain talkers,
Grass anchored gravel,
Perched on a watery breeze, sand piping,
Chained to another world,
Ferry bondage and moneyed meanders,
Bused to the beaches,
Pining trees, aching for halyard cloth,
Salt sputtered racing faces,
Back slapping crossings,
Farewell to the castles of sand,
Bucketed windmill dreams,
Decks of chairs and washing weed,
Competing cords and piloted shortcuts,
Struggling bold Bass braces,
Across the juggling jigsaw sea.

No Coals

Rattling over the high-level span,
A peaceful southerner with an empty hod,
Eying a proverbial quote,
Upon the enduring spine of Stephenson,
Rails riding over walkers,
Unguided machines stray from channel bounds,
The discharging fade of grounded fortifications,
Top hats buried and mislaid,
Nothing sliding off to sea, sparkling wine lubrication,
Cheering docks and gloomy locks, corroded closed,
Gantry braces sent for scrap,
No fleeing the back-to-back,
Tearful towers and monumental substitution,
Propped black powder slowly rises,
Breathing energy into a starving nation,
The resolute lovers, metal gripped,
Slippery sides shun the drawing moon,
Those gangly cranes have no regard for spring,
The neap drops a dull future on the wharf,
Recurring shovels persist,
Pressing small hope, floating freight, visiting home,
Burning their precious cargo in far-flung stacks,
Returning swiftly before the need is fulfilled,
By new world diggers and fabricators.

Another Yawning Morning

The crimson cream creature, crawled to a standstill,
Sweeping streamlines, every excursion recounted,
Carrying countless miles,
Primed for a bitter morning jaunt,
Bursting dampness, antique smoke,
Preceding travelers, scenting shining floors,
Inebriated night owls, social drinkers,
Retreating to vibrant seats,
Outings to the circus and suffering zoo,
Downhill dashes, to sea stroked shores,
Climbing towards metropolitan lights,
Another yawning morning,
Packed with porridge and sandwich satchels,
Lunchtime odors, straight after breakfast,
Above the wheels, passing morning sickness,
Scrubbed pearly teeth, buttoned right up,
Longing for the warm afternoon return,
Strewn winter coats, opportunistic study,
Forgotten benches and sluggish teachers,
Evading the laws of the day,
The icy dawn left for tomorrow.

The winding Frome

Emerging from the seeded attic,
Drowsy Evershot, continual tears,
Forded and repelling, daily invaders,
Hiking downstairs through jade pastures,
Soft white rock and cupped butter,
Carrying primitive hopes,
Far off fine china, ridge railings,
Cleaved from a scraped and packed course,
Substituting work for play,
Thrown throngs of gleaming synthetic toys,
Sending the nomadic mink scampering,
Skirting the lethargic sun worshipers,
Coiled in venomous knots,
Flowing in the sludge, an era of ice,
With the territorial army of sewer mouthed mullet,
Surface filters, leaping prizes, netted by night,
Under the watchful eyes of the Durotriges,
Shrouded frigid air, rolling with field creases,
Lifting odorous muggy hay and locked livestock,
Dispatching night visitors on a spontaneous adventure,
Banked with the retreating edge,
Awaiting the morning surge.

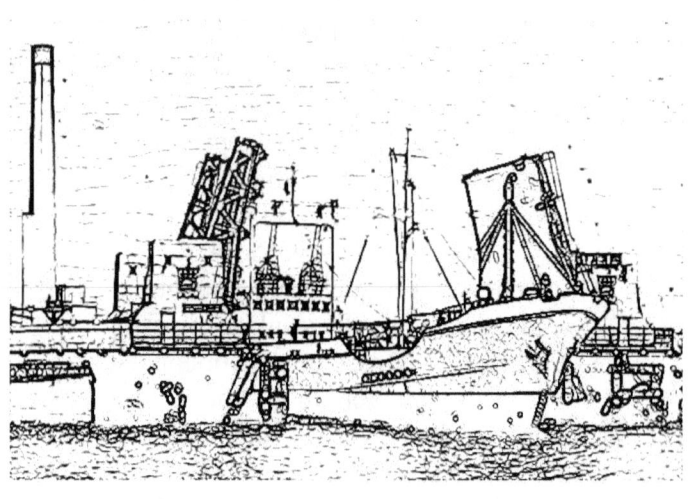

Horace and the Lifting Bridge

Biting cold chewed the hard-edged wharf,
Floating hopes tethered and rowed,
The leisurely ebb, slapping greenheart poles,
Slippery backed mussels and a promised return,
The slight man in the bascule bridge,
Three hundred tons raised, a one handed wheel,
Herculean mechanics, tiled insignia,
Horace the rigger gripping, rapidly recurring steps,
Frosted fastenings, havoc for the last gunner on deck,
Nose dripping cold, diving plans deferred,
Money for a mooring, some glassy yacht,
Detained all seasons, six days use,
Slipping away with a head full of knowledge,
Passing the masses, freshly sawn sappy timber,
Taking the straight road for the last time,
Seeing the smoking heaps, quitting a lifetime habit,
No more coughing smutty smolder for Swedish lungs,
Swallowed frigid water, a warm shore bath,
Tough wire rope unspliced, taking a toll,
On cold brine wintered fingers.

Mythical Titans

Mythical titans tower over basin bricks,
Former custodians of unsinkable guarantees,
Balanced and begging for a tolerant world,
Indelibly marking the trust of a generation,
Upon a continually changing sky,
White stars and weaponry,
Ravenous kings propelling the hopes of queens,
Ancient antagonists, hauled to an anvil table,
Bulleted hot thrown fasteners, soft tissue exposed,
Fusing colossal conundrums with optimistic iron,
Single dimensional symbols, obeyed collective wishes
Blackened salt streams over fiery hands,
Exhausted armor, shifted and shuffled,
Resting in the scarlet puzzles of Pakenham Street,
Slamming the door on continual clamor,
Still tasting the metallic inferno,
Prizing open the jaws of the sandbar,
Gliding out on Lagan and Lough,
Swimming for the guiding stream,
Dreams of dancing on moonlit gin,
Partying passages to the other side,
Where the lady stands waiting,
Lighting the advance with her burning torch,
Gazing towards meager suggestions,
Promises emerging from a distant horizon.

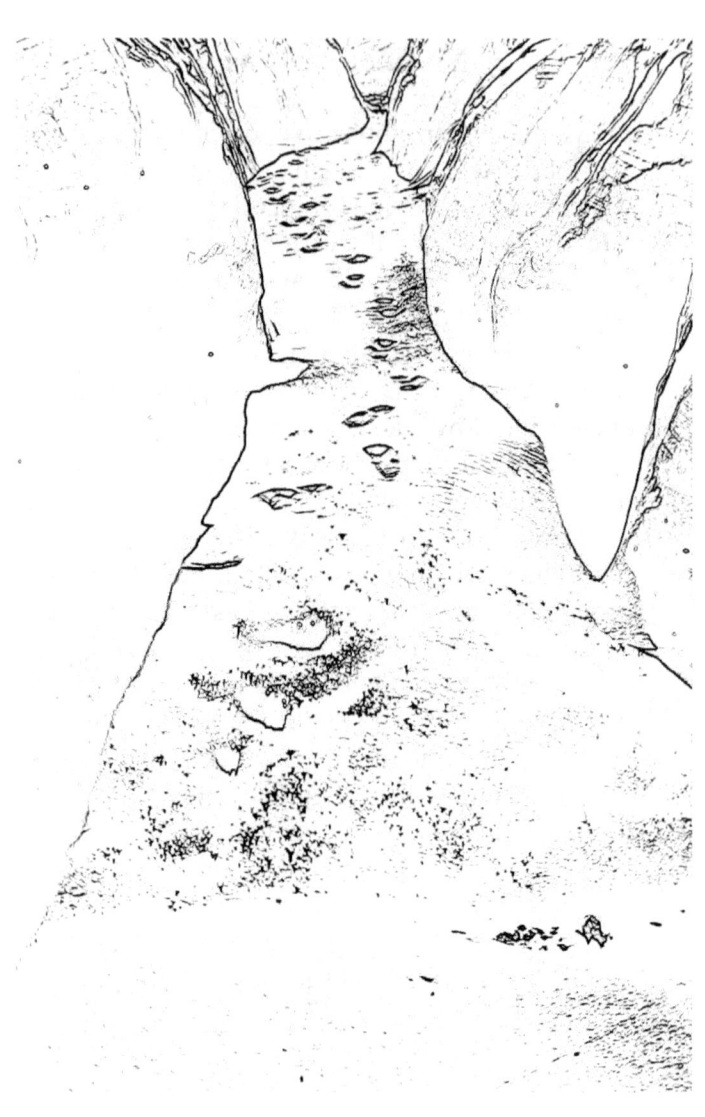

Sahra to Sahel

Plummeting from the heights of the walled Atlas,
Coursing and risking a southward jaunt,
Into the baked backdrop of misplaced meanders,
Secreted branches, oasis dreams,
Liberated aquifers, fighting for the surface,
Satisfying our dusty thirst,
Some linger cloaked for a new adventure,
The blazing orb, denies today's passage,
Whilst winded corrugations,
Swathe my return with doubt,
Confusing the misguided, journeying forward,
Not a trace of promising infrastructure,
Blocked by the daily growth of sand mountains,
Feeding on the dusted bones,
Those preceding conquest driven slaves,
That persistent wind,
Carrying not a drop, for seed or bud,
Trophy fruits or morsels of expectation,
A few pointless teasing clouds,
Pipedreams of a downpour,
No possibility of reaching up,
Wringing their white necks,
Drawing a drop of cloud blood
towards the desiccated floor,
Just those shadowy dark patches, more conundrums,
Throwing circles around the heart,
Staging posts for unheard prayers,
The jade and gentle Sahel, absorbs our minds,
Gesturing towards a welcome Saharan reprieve.

Scrumping

Seasoned leaf shielded targets,
Shined in the summer sun,
Ready for plucking,
Glimpsed from the other side of soaring barriers,
A mountainous climb, a worthy feast,
Strolling towards the prize, straightforward enough,
The cherry-faced fuming farmer, a surprise,
Cocked double barrels, our direction,
Upping the pace, making for a dash and a dive,
Under and over,
Hearts through hoops, joining jugular necks,
Sidestepping sky scraping hurdles,
Added backpacks, bursting with trouble,
Yearning for a succulent experience,
Stinging rock salt, reddened legs,
Hoping the palpitations would slow,
The guilt of adventure dropping,
From sun browned summer faces,
Returning home for tea and parental explanations.

Loch Life

Pallid lobsters grazed upon Precambrian shelves,
Bothering vulnerable visitors,
With a pinch and wrench,
Snaking beside the scalloped beaches,
Briefly netted, sprouting lonely tubes,
Visiting armlet piers, strung into the darkest deep,
Shielding whisky drenched shores from invasion,
As a dram or more sedated fingers,
Leaving blue toes sitting, for hours in icy water,
Longing for gilled grilling victims,
The humble moorland hosts, scones and sports,
Broad oaks gone, firing the iron of city railings,
Deciduous splendor, exchanged for pastel heather,
A clear view to bored basking life and lonesome isles,
Lost under Mesolithic feet,
Roaming in earth stirring sunsets,
Consuming the last of the stream,
Savoring the warmth,
Atlantic lungs overflowing, lazing in loch life,
Dreaming of emerging giants
and fiery cinder causeways.

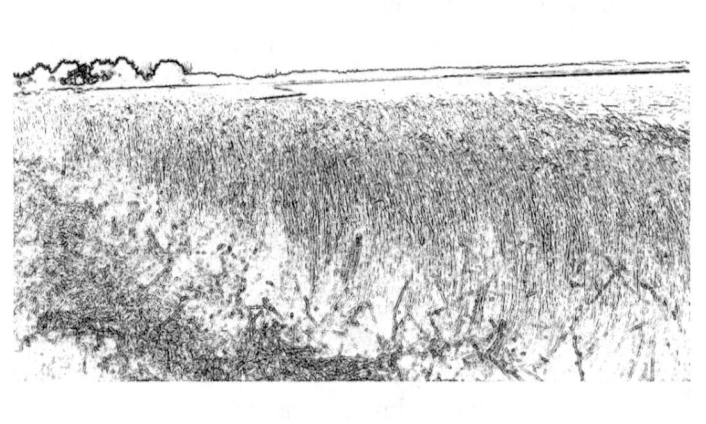

Mud and Shale

Time to unplug the grimy green bathtub,
Torrents rush under the locomotive-topped span,
Weeded worn keels reveal, resting rusted iron,
Hidden hope anchors, the weakest link,
Daily beatings of salted solutions
and barnacle builders,
Broken boats scattered among the exiled weeds,
Bulging air, sulfur sludge,
Clinging to deserted damp, dirtied thatching reeds,
No lofty prospects beyond their muddy roots,
Heavy old blue vessels relax,
Stranded on stretching mooring manacles,
Wading through the suction of suffocating mud,
Grating vulnerable shins, sharp shale and buried being,
Scuttling greens on sideway diversions,
Evading inquisitive stares and ambushing nets,
Thirsty algae strains for high water,
Pegged on washing line ropes,
Stranded flounders hold on,
Veiled in mud tone and orange,
Waiting for water,
Mud, shale and buoyancy restored.

Semi-detached

Spongy carrot carpet hugged precipitous stairs,
Rolling edges and a chilling climb,
Boarded banisters, resistant dust,
Nothing to grab on the way down,
Never looking back, going up,
Worrying rhymes, old men and stairs,
Changing mile high light bulbs,
Competing with silk ceiling spiders,
Shiny bathrooms, hanging chains,
Walled water and musty sweet rising damp,
Jericho and a slow filled bath,
Colors contradicted, thirty years reworked,
Organized lawns, cement solid borders,
A halcyon plot, between the rotten rows and washing,
Tinted hydrangeas and hyacinth margins,
Disruptive hollyhock fences, plump berry strays,
Unruly rhubarb, battling the manicured green haulm,
Boiled ants and salted slugs, a garden holocaust,
Wicked weeds and established order,
Optimistic dreams of hearted lettuce,
Polished crimson globes, semi-detached fruit.

Rhondda

Engraving dissent trekked the vociferous ravine,
Ancient table servings set in a different time,
Towards the Fawr and Fach,
Stone apparatus and arrows,
Solitary blades, no tough valley steel,
Deep in a chiseled landscape of passé promises,
Modest people, nourishing a vast machine,
Perpetually waning, never emerging,
Coughing up a half-life underground,
A million miles from technology,
Humans no longer the shaded ants, waiting for rain,
Tunneling worms, without a protesting word,
Secretly praying for the children above,
Longing for them to wear white, everyday,
Sitting behind a desk, free roaming the surface,
Raising the odd spirit with harmonic optimism,
Percentages gripping the rest,
Ignoring adversity, the struggles of yesterday,
No more burning of the black stuff,
Those youthful hopes, drift on past,
Plugged ears not hearing the ground,
Fathers and friends, sit on callused hands,
Wishing they had stayed below and planted flowers.

The Auction

Crumpled cash tightly gripped
in desiccated winter hands,
Anxiously ready for the right one,
The heavy wooden doors parting,
Revealing a slightly scruffy offering,
Revved high by an enthusiastic teenager,
Without a license,
Skidded to a deafening halt for the money changers,
The microphone man spools a description,
Placed under starting orders, the battle commences,
Low fidelity words, ambiguous meaning,
Syrupy tea excitingly spilled, grease printed china,
Handed platters, brilliant bread sandwiches,
Arms thrown high for a desirable gem,
Packed with padded rust, sanded to near perfection,
A new topcoat, no reverse and one ancient owner,
Never run without the clutching choke,
A smattering of synthetic scent,
Disguising dog-walking carpets,
The scorching standing stove roars,
The night air swells with cigarettes
and profitable plans,
Tomorrows doubled money,
Two bald tires, well washed,
A little sputter and a need for ten more,
Leaving every lung noxious,
With the fumes of cold running.

Mountain View

Frost shattered slated stands rise above the daily flow,
A somber shrouded hymnal,
Wedged on a puzzling step,
A shuttered place of requests,
With no prospective patron,
Prayers whispered to the wind, granted on the go,
Holding on to life, bathing with crisp falling silver,
Never yielding to mineral impediment,
Snaking over smooth tar, crossing binary lines,
Lifting the black boots of transitory travelers,
Cascading towards an emerald collage,
Bouncing on bundles of rummaging wool,
Vociferous hawks and misplaced rodents,
Floating over a deceitful drop,
Leaning with the rigid breeze,
Thrashing along the winding paths,
Never knowing what lies ahead,
Underpowered two-wheelers,
Overwhelmed wrong-sided rovers,
Meandering muddied muck scrapers,
Mindful of cows with bursting udders,
Unseen by night riding passers, dilated pupils focused,
Weakening white rays, drifting driving darkness,
Dreaming of home fires,
Soft comfortable couches and no mountain view.

Troubled Father

Backward surges forever restricted,
Reluctant conformists, curtailed tides,
Lowered upper reaches, broken industrial backs,
Dry docks drenched, watery yards dehydrated,
Bartered for simple one eyed pleasures,
Sky grating probes and concertinas,
The dumbest barges have voices,
Lighters lug the weighty world,
Mislaid bodies and dumped disorder,
Pressed off course, secreted from view,
Decisions handed down,
Beneath a proudly sounding clock,
Towers lift and fall with newly severed heads,
Hindered fighting ships,
Back dropped banks of misunderstanding,
The tourists trip on cobbled edges,
Clouded beyond East India,
Tilbury tipping the scales for China,
Borrowed bricks for rebuilt garden walls,
Paving the way to a new face,
Those absent barrow boys, big boxed off the curve,
The rest cocooned in mocking assumption,
Troubled, as father continues to sweat.

Ivorian Hope

The dark storm skipped over the Ivorian sea,
Passing the faded pastels of colonial diehards,
Softly swaying balancers rested,
Cooling the lofty fruits of labor,
Losing altitude for a moment,
Counterpart stilts, enduring a lifetime wait,
Beneath a succulent emerald canopy,
Praying for a long taxi or muddied bus,
Smiling corners brightening, a simple world,
Frowning outlawed, small screens absent,
A grin for free, pennies to lend a hand,
Feeding the folly circles,
Deliverance for someone,
Dodging the shoeless ramblers,
Fumigating humid crops,
Dispatched to a waiting world of disturbed dentists,
Delicious fodder for sweet teeth,
Barefoot traffic brushed, speeding limousines,
Silhouettes move in time,
With contorted ochre offspring,
Powdered drums, tinkering with earthen ears,
Shapely night shadows, stroll city pavements,
Joining the insect survivors,
Their drawing tubes honed,
Carefully searching for a succulent stranger.

The King's Daughter

Grazing plateaus gazed down,
Drifting with martyrs and dark water currents,
Veiled saints and sacrifices, rising up, folding down,
Carved emeralds, concealing darkness beneath,
The lost souls of a shadow stacking generation,
Fuelling another realm without recompense,
Spent ironmasters and cruel fuel fires,
Bondage debt and trucking tactics,
Enslaved champions, trapped no more,
Ready to ride with the Watling Street crowd,
Voiceless voids readied for ingested pride,
Dreaming of brick departures in bitter soot,
Swarming voices, breathing resonated radiance,
Threadbare seams, nourishment for choking houses,
Blasting and fulling breaks,
Modest fires and woolen bleats,
Sent to some far off place, ready to wear,
The final fragile fossils packed,
Fueling those nation-building furnaces,
Bridging and skyscraping,
Sometimes some primitive support,
Bolted to the earth, stalking new tenants,
Forgetting the woes of the king's daughter.

The Smoke

Damp fogged lungs traveled on coal-smoked air,
Congregated corners,
Pyramid brick and mortar ruins,
Fissured streets side stepped,
Heaven and hearth hung thirty feet high,
Handing optimism to pitching peddlers
and parallel parkers,
Tall reds wrestled with busy blacks,
Skirting space on parallel strips,
Discontented cargo slipped by unseen,
Snorted vapor and weighted water,
Melancholy monochrome, smooth silver,
Guiding brilliance as Morpheus strayed for a moment,
Blotting memories of antagonists
and insurmountable costs,
Lost humble brothers and absent children,
Opening on time with everything formerly on hold,
The end of hostilities and closed for lunch,
For a minute, the time was theirs,
Retaking life,
In a world of trampled tyrants and smoke.

Ship Canals and Red Bricks

Sea link locks and taller ships,
Mersey skirting ramparts,
Doorstep oceans, sleazy clocked corners,
Bombsite flicks and packing places,
Strange ways to call,
Barred from the rest, compartment homes,
Industrial branches and collecting books,
Pennies pinched, paltry payments,
Snoring red brick soaring,
Fruitless mills, unlocked thrills,
Rainy days and bagged wind,
Ragged trade and rusted tops,
Threaded station stops,
Far Eastern destinations,
Cloth ears and celebration days.

Three Hundred and Ninety Nine

The striking majestic arch
is out of the landscape forever,
A lumbering giant toying with the old chessboard,
had won that piece,
Crushing it in his cruel hands,
Hastily pitching it to the side,
An irate victor,
With a gleeful expression from ear to ear,
Looking down from above, speculating,
Whether we would notice,
The somber passing of an icon,
Taking a black rattler to the steps,
Of some impassive shocking slab,
Purposeful and completely meaningless,
Far in the shadows of hope, the glory of the Midland,
The gothic grandiose guarantee of Saint Pancras,
Three hundred and ninety nine miles ahead,

Across the terrain, once understood,
Chattering over conduits,
Rumbling into the wedged earth,
Through the stifled blackness of bricked tubes,
Faltering for virtually every week of the year,
Disrupting the bowing sea, nodding somnolent heads,
Roughing their rigid necks back and forth,
The only link with Finnieston
and silent Clydebank cranes,
Reassuring them with the hiss of dense air,
Awakened by unbridled brakes,
The drumming drizzle on lung fogged glass,
Approaching the end of the line,
Dreading the loss of a dry haven,
Left to linger under Heilanman's umbrella,
Waiting for the worst to pass
and Argyle Street to beckon.

The Guardian

Emblematic ashen precipices sweep from the depths,
Natures score driven, flanking foreign turfs,
Frosted swimmers and hectic traffic watching,
Pinched in a straw funnel, released again into the flow,
The guardian trench,
Blocking optimistic tunnels and dry feet,
Libraries packed with dusty plans,
Precarious bridges and balloon jaunts,
A bobbing flotilla prepared for attack,
Swiftly fogged in thick, an ambiguous itinerary,
Redeemers in little ships travel, rescuing lost warriors,
Here to there, back to sanctuary,
Set for another day of high expectations,
Dogged with clouded mist,
Scraped off the horizon draft,
Thrown in the course of chugging iron,
Ambling and unfurled cloth,
Mystifying the spinning compass,
Deadlocked with a walled eyed skull
and fellow explorers,
Sitting in a salty shower, fully dressed,
Bracing for a hearty crunch,
Praying for a timely escape.

Tar and Tie

Tar and tie, aired bitumen runs,
Cricket ratchets in labor crushed rock,
Hissing silver, time to leap,
Black broom crackers, humming gorse wounded,
Muddled life junctions and pointed handles,
Oven baked rust, paper tailings,
Bolted heaps, waiting weeded dozens,
Thorny parts with barbed competition,
Miles of tension, drawn in,
First and second, third standing,
Arms down, waiting and dark flooding,
Up and pointing, charged departures,
Sluggish thunder and a lightening down run.

The Sitting Room

The furniture rudely exposed its back,
To the rest of the sitting room,
An ugly floral design,
An intimate connection with the curtains,
Ivy damp crept the walls,
Interfering with pasted paper,
Monotonous patterns, three-dimensional aspects,
Tainted ginger carpet, bitter air and abundant ash,
Art off the shelf, straight on the wall,
The gypsy dancer timed, with the brass mantle clock,
Rotating calendars, calmly gesturing,
Passing time with television and lava lamp,
Struggling for undivided attention,
Swiftly the distracters overwhelm,
The great human regulators, adapt the occupants,
Components in one colossal chronometer,
Tedious competitive conversation chimes,
Masking the hum of Saturday sport,
The ticking heartburning menu served,
Washed with pails of dated beer,
Hand grabbing insipid food, insulted stomachs,
Throwing a spanner into the movement,
Liberated acid, sent for repair,
Fortunate this time,
One day this ghastly space would no longer host,
Partitioned hell and timepieces,
Grinding to a stop.

The Unyielding Zebra

High street stripes and no barricade,
A rapid onslaught,
Screaming wheels and horror faces,
Lost at the hands of a frantic young man,
The crosser not so swift,
Weighted by the chattels of existence,
Machine creased news,
Tinned snuff and warming woodbines,
Scarves for drafts, a bitter weathered coat,
Reusable shopping bags, an outing every Thursday,
Lining up and collecting a pittance, for years paid in,
Trifles for battles fought,
Time in rotting mire filled trenches,
A dash through the flowered fields of the French,
Watery offensives, barbed wire beaches,
Norman shores and goal practice for the enemy,
A loaf of bread and a cup of sugared tea,
Small treats once a week,
Soon the bloodied tabloid floated under foot,
Rising and curling through winter space,
An extra bulletin not yet printed,
Clearly inking the stopped press,
Two world wars, sadly lost in a high street battle,
Extinguished cigarettes, bittersweet dust,
No more pensions or weekly shopping,
Another soldier lost in daily combat.

The Harbor

Sun dried bladderwrack,
Loafs with the warm rock crystals,
Hitching hands and jocular foot traffic,
Shattered razors and spent tails,
Amusing inquisitive beaks,
Wet green fingers gripping the tidal mire,
Oblique sand sentries,
Standing to attention at prohibitive intervals,
Interrupting a faultless view from folding chairs,
Out to the buzz cut green of stationary masses,
Aquatic dreams of miniature liners,
Diminutive charges seldom visited,
Viewed proudly from iconic summer shells,
Rowed upon the planned shore,
Mossy concrete and regimental grass,
Drinking and brewing, sandwiches devoured,
Traveling towers of steel, making close passes,
Underwater cuttings, scraping through,
Stirring the nerves of quivering brethren,
Beleaguered beaches and the loss of frozen ice,
Tears to the loser, smiles to a wagging stray,
Shuffling shame trusts modesty, to Turkish cotton,
Time to prize their progeny from the surf,
Salted sand tantrums, compete with the hungry gulls,
Bribed by sugary stuff
and tomorrows promised return.

Relegated to the Guards Van

Cycling halfway once more,
Relegated to the guards van,
Wedged in a rattling cage, with the last door to slam,
Timber floors and fifty years of thrashing,
The same old rhythm, fresh passengers,
Stilted splinters, not first-class cushions,
Traveling amongst the dogs and boxed birds,
The easy way home,
Rabid pets and lost leg messages,
Rising and falling with distorted mailbags,
Brown telephone bills, plain white letters,
Parcels and unfinished walls,
Bolted and locked at running speed,
Shadow steam or steadfast diesel,
Push button launches, weighted coal,
Blackened faces, shovel-blistered hands,
Tanked to the top and guzzling,
Pressed vapor and idle axes,
Locked down brakes and futile escapes.

ABOUT THE AUTHOR

Nicholas Price is a poet whose work has been published through a series of bespoke and mainstream publications and books.

With a legacy of work now collated and published in several new titles, bringing a unique poetic style and perspective to a wide range of subjects enjoyed by all readers and ages.

His poetry, writings and photographic work have been exhibited at key events and institutions. The acclaimed collection titled *Cleared Hot!* – a photographic story and essay - was acquired by one of the world's most prestigious institutions, the United States Library of Congress.

OTHER AVAILABLE TITLES

America is a way of life and a state of mind, to be savored and discovered.
Nicholas Price celebrates this beauty and diversity through his poetic artistry. His journeys take us from the Bridges to Manhattan to the pioneer trails of the
West Coast and beyond.

Nicholas Price takes us on a poetic journey through childhood and life experience.
Nostalgic, amusing and a must read for those who sometimes question; "whatever happened to the world we grew up in?"

Forgotten Holiday is one book to keep amongst your own treasure trove of memories.

Nicholas Price presents his frank and sometimes humorous poetic thoughts and observations on life.
From social and political change to the hopes of us all.

Described as "a refreshing new voice in poetry", these works are timeless and reflective of the world we once knew and the one we have become.

How would you describe being in love to someone who has never experienced it?
Poet Nicholas Price pens the human storms of desire, heartbreak and devotion.
The distant yearning to unyielding passion, absence and infidelity, grief and solitude, those erratic and chaotic emotions we call love.

Tough Tribe
ToughTribe.com

Buy All Four Books At Our Special Collector Set Price

www.ToughTribe.com
Also available at Amazon.com and all other fine bookstores